19.95

Peru

by Joyce Markovics

Consultant: Karla Ruiz
Teacher's College, Columbia University
New York, New York

BEARPORT
PUBLISHING

New York, New York

Credits

Cover © Andy Dean Photography/Shutterstock and Anton_Ivanov/Shutterstock; 3, © Dario Lo Presti/Shutterstock; 4, © Anton_Ivanov/Shutterstock; 5L, © Carlos E. Santa Maria/Shutterstock; 5R, © Bartosz Hadyniak/iStock; 7, © ostill/Shutterstock; 8, © javarman/Shutterstock; 9, © Tomasz Resiak/iStock; 10L, © allinvisuality/iStock; 10–11, © Mike Treglia/Shutterstock; 12T, © Dirk Ercken/Shutterstock; 12B, © Anan Kaewkhammul/Shutterstock; 13, © Edwin Butter/Shutterstock; 14–15, © Mark Skalny/Shutterstock; 16, © Courtesy Architect of the Capitol; 17, © Carlos Mora/Alamy Stock Photo; 18–19, © Fotos593/Shutterstock; 19B, © Vadim Petrakov/Shutterstock; 20, © Carlos Mora/Alamy Stock Photo; 21, © Bartosz Hadyniak/iStock; 22, © Hans Geel/Shutterstock; 23, © Byelikova Oksana/Shutterstock; 24, © sunsinger/Shutterstock; 25, © Christian Vinces/Shutterstock; 26, © Bartosz Hadyniak/iStock; 26–27, © PavelSvoboda/Shutterstock; 28B, © Ozgur Guvene/Shutterstock; 28–29, © Bartosz Hadyniak/iStock; 30T, © Anton_Ivanov/Shutterstock and Christian Vinces/Shutterstock; 30B, © suebmtl/Shutterstock; 31(T to B), © Fotos593/Shutterstock, © javarman/Shutterstock, © ostill/Shutterstock, © ostill/Shutterstock, © Mike Treglia/Shutterstock, and © Fotos593/Shutterstock; 32, © Neftali/Shutterstock.

Publisher: Kenn Goin
Senior Editor: Joyce Tavolacci
Creative Director: Spencer Brinker
Design: Debrah Kaiser
Photo Researcher: Olympia Shannon

Library of Congress Cataloging-in-Publication Data

Names: Markovics, Joyce L., author.
Title: Peru / by Joyce Markovics.
Description: New York, New York : Bearport Publishing, [2017] | Series:
   Countries we come from | Includes bibliographical references and index. |
   Audience: Ages 6–10._
Identifiers: LCCN 2016006799 (print) | LCCN 2016007059 (ebook) | ISBN
   9781944102739 (library binding) | ISBN 9781944102890 (ebook)
Subjects: LCSH: Peru—Juvenile literature.
Classification: LCC F3408.5 .M353 2017 (print) | LCC F3408.5 (ebook) | DDC
   985—dc23
LC record available at http://lccn.loc.gov/2016006799

For more information, write to Bearport Publishing Company, Inc., 45 West 21st Street, Suite 3B, New York, New York 10010. Printed in the United States of America.

10 9 8 7 6 5 4 3 2 1

Contents

BREATHTAKING

Ancient

Friendly

Peru is a large country in South America.

It's twice as big as the state of Texas.

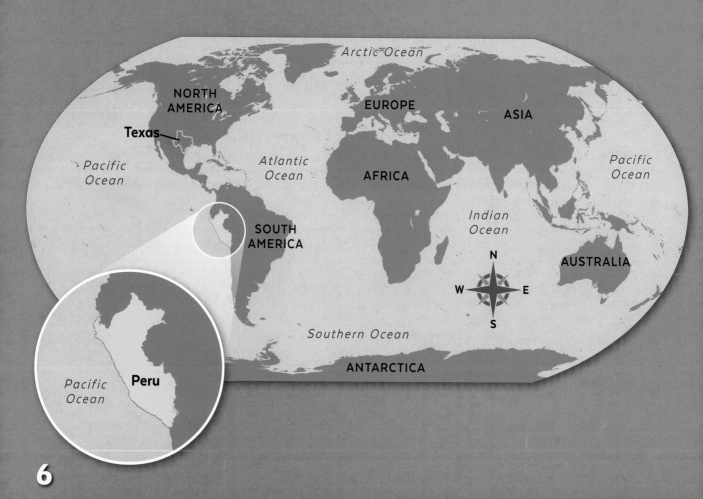

More than 30 million people live in Peru.

Peru has a very long **coast**.
Much of the land is dry and dusty.

Peru's coast stretches along the Pacific Ocean for 1,500 miles (2,414 km)!

Not far from the coast
is a strip of tall mountains.

They are called the Andes.

Andes
Mountains

A huge jungle covers about half of Peru.

The jungle is called the Amazon.

It's the world's largest **rain forest**!

rain forest flower

The Amazon River flows through the rain forest.

11

Thousands of animals live in the Amazon.

Colorful frogs rest in trees.

Jaguars roam the forest floor.

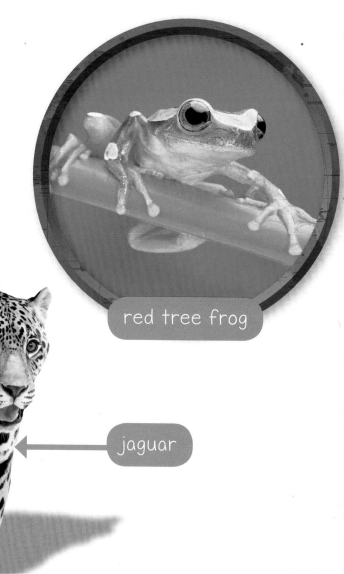

red tree frog

jaguar

emperor tamarin

Many kinds of monkeys
live in the Amazon, too.

13

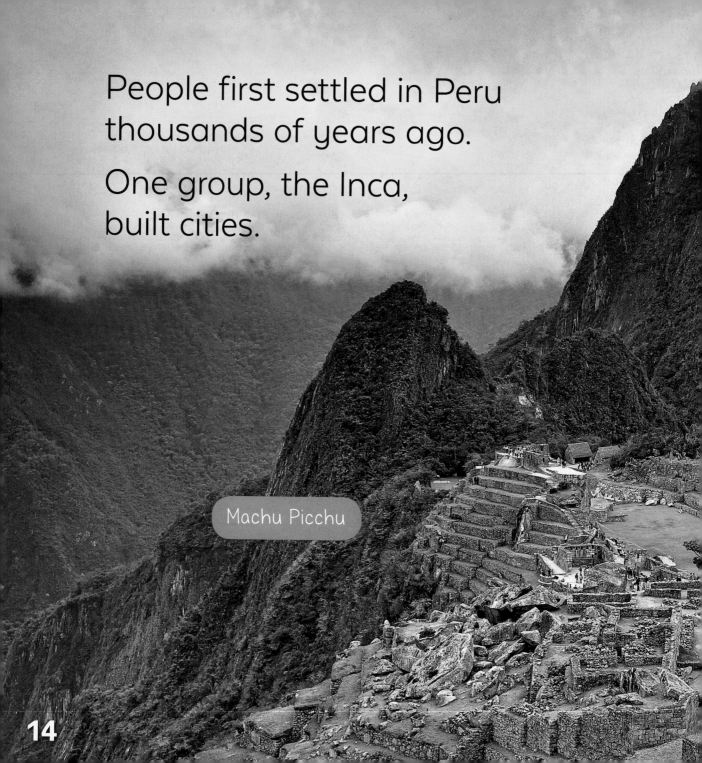

People first settled in Peru thousands of years ago.

One group, the Inca, built cities.

Machu Picchu

The Inca city of Machu Picchu (MAH-choo PEE-choo) is high in the mountains.

Thousands of people visit the ancient city each year.

The Spanish came to Peru in the 1500s.

They ruled for hundreds of years.

In 1821, Peru became a free country.

Each year, Peruvians celebrate their **independence** on July 28.

Today, most Peruvians live in cities.

The largest city is Lima.

It's also the **capital** of Peru.

There's a park in Lima where hundreds of cats live!

The main language in Peru is Spanish.

This is how you say *book* in Spanish:
Libro (LEE-broh)

This is how you say *child*:
Niño (NEEN-yoh)

Many Peruvians also speak the Inca language Quechua (KEESH-wah).

21

Peruvian food is delicious!

Along the coast, seafood is popular.

In the mountains, people enjoy potatoes and meat.

a seafood dish called ceviche (say–VEE–chay)

Potatoes come from Peru. Now they're grown all over the world!

Peruvians love soccer.

It's the **national** sport.

Everyone enjoys kicking the ball!

Surfing is also a popular sport in Peru.

Peru is known for its beautiful **textiles**.

People raise alpacas for their wool.

The wool is then made into colorful cloth.

a woman weaving cloth

Alpacas are related
to llamas and camels.

Music fills the air in parts of Peru.

People play panpipes and flutes.

Peruvians enjoy the sweet sounds!

People blow into panpipes to play them.

Peruvian flute

Fast Facts

Capital city: Lima

Population of Peru: More than 30 million

Main languages: Spanish, Quechua, and Aymara

Money: Nuevo Sol

Major religion: Roman Catholic

Neighboring countries: Ecuador, Colombia, Brazil, Bolivia, and Chile

Cool Fact: Seabirds called Humboldt penguins nest in desert areas along Peru's coast.

capital (KAP-uh-tuhl) a city where a country's government is based

coast (KOHST) land that runs along an ocean

independence (in-di-PEN-duhnss) freedom from outside control

national (NASH-uh-nuhl) having to do with a whole country

rain forest (RAYN FOR-ist) a warm, wet place where many trees grow

textiles (TEK-stiles) cloth that has been woven or knitted

Index

Read More

Landau, Elaine. *Peru (True Books: Countries).* New York: Children's Press (2000).

Newman, Sandra. *The Inca Empire (True Books: Ancient Civilizations).* New York: Scholastic (2010).

Learn More Online

To learn more about Peru, visit
www.bearportpublishing.com/CountriesWeComeFrom

About the Author

Joyce Markovics lives along the Hudson River in a very old house. She dreams of visiting the cloud-covered ancient city of Machu Picchu.